The Proverbs Character C

Proverbs People Workbook #1

Slothful vs. Diligent
Righteous vs. Wicked
The Five Fools
The Wise Man
The Prudent Man
Liar vs. Faithful Witness

By Rick and Marilyn Boyer

Illustrated by Kate Boyer Brown

Second Printing 2005
Third Printing 2007
Fourth Printing 2010

The Learning Parent
2430 Sunnymeade Rd.
Rustburg, VA 24588

Dear Parents:

This workbook is the offshoot of a project we created for our own children. We believe that Proverbs, the book of fatherly wisdom, is a treasury of child training principles. A study of character types in the book is a tremendously valuable exercise because it calls the child's attention to Godly character and lists the attributes of each type, giving the child a basis for evaluating his own character and responding to others wisely.

The application questions on the page following the short-answer sections are designed to help the child think about the life applications of the principles behind the character qualities. We think they will be the most helpful if you discuss them with your child.

We also recommend that you use the fun quiz as a supplement to your family devotional time in addition to having your child work through it on his own. You may want to cut out the quiz pages from other Proverbs Workbooks to make a notebook of fun questions for family time quizzes.

We encourage you to have your children memorize some of the verses listed for study, especially the one on the **coloring page** at the end of each section. That page can be transferred onto a T-shirt as a visible reminder of a Biblical principle by simply having the child color **on the reverse side of the page** with fabric crayons and then ironing the page onto the front of the shirt. Detailed instructions are given on the back of a package of fabric crayons.

Look up the verses below and write answers to the questions.

The Sluggard

(Lazy, slothful)

Proverbs 6:6-11

1. What animal can teach a sluggard about diligence?

____

2. Does an ant have to be forced to work or does he do it by his own choice?

____

____

____

3. Do ants look ahead and prepare for future needs? _______________________________________

4. Do you think a sluggard would look ahead and prepare for future needs? ______________________________

5. What does a sluggard like to do?

____

6. What happens to the sluggard in the end?

____

____

____

____

Proverbs 10:26

7. If you sent a lazy person to do something for you, would he make you glad you had sent him? ___________________

Proverbs 12:24

8. If a lazy man and a diligent man work in the same place, which one is more likely to become a leader?

____

Proverbs 12:27

9. Does a slothful man finish the job of cooking and eating the game he brought home from hunting? _______________

Proverbs 18:9

10. A man who is lazy in his work is like a man who does what? ____

Proverbs 13:4

11. How is a sluggard's soul different from the soul of a diligent man?

____

____

Proverbs 15:19

12. Does a sluggard find that his life is easy?

____

Proverbs 19:15

13. Does laziness make a person sleepy?

____

14. Will a slothful person have plenty to eat?

____

Proverbs 19:24

15. Would a sluggard jump up from the table to go get something he needed? Would he gladly cut up meat for his little brothers and sisters?

____

Proverbs 20:4

16. Does a sluggard keep his garden plowed?

____

17. Does the sluggard work now because he knows he will need to eat later? ______________________________

18. What will the sluggard have to do at harvest time, when his neighbors are gathering in their crops?

____

Proverbs 21:25,26

19. Does the sluggard have what he needs? Why or why not?

____

____

____

____

20. Do you think a righteous man would be lazy?

____

21. Do you think a lazy man likes to give things to others?

____

Proverbs 22:13

22. Does the slothful man make up excuses to keep from going to work? ________________________________

23. Do you think most people would believe his excuses? Why or why not?

____

Proverbs 24:30-34

24. Does a lazy man have much understanding? (verse 30)

____

25. Would it be easy to work in a field like this? Why or why not? (verse 31)

____

____

____

____

____

____

26. Can animals get into this field and eat the fruit? Why? (verse 31)

____

____

27. What should we do when we see the results of laziness? (verse 32)

____

28. What lessons could you learn by looking at a lazy man's field?

____

____

____

____

29. Could you grow much food in a field like the one you read about here?

____

30. Does it take a lot of laziness to cause problems, or only a little? (verse 33)

____

Proverbs 26:13-16

31. Is the lazy man careful to tell the truth?

____

32. Is the lazy man quick to get out of bed in the morning?

____

33. Do you think the sluggard would eat his meals without wasting time?

____

34. Does the slothful man realize he is being foolish?

____

35. Does he have respect for wise people?

____

An Example of Slothfulness

Dean and Rickey were very sad. Trips to Granddad's farm were supposed to be fun. But today, things had taken a bad turn. The evening before, the boys had come back from the pond with four nice catfish they had caught. They had put them in an old dish pan full of water out beside the well, planning to clean them after supper. But when supper was over they were full and tired from digging worms, walking through the fields, and fishing. So they decided the fish would be just fine in the dish pan until morning. They would clean them then.

But now it was morning and the two boys stood looking down into the dish pan, which was still full of water but no fish. They had all been taken during the night. Their father stepped out of the house and closed the screen door behind him.

"What's wrong, boys?" he asked.

"We've lost our fish," Dean explained.

"Somebody stole them!" Rickey added.

Dad looked thoughtful. "I think I can guess who got them," he said.

Both boys looked up. "Who? Who did it?" they wanted to know.

"I'd say it was the cats. They love fish."

"You mean the barn cats?" Rickey asked, his eyes wide. "I thought cats hated water. We didn't think they'd bother fish in the pan."

"You're right, son, they do hate water. But they love fish so much that they'll dip into a pan like that and snatch a fish quickly with a front paw. Then they drag it away to the barn and eat it."

"Why, those rotten cats! That was a dirty trick!" said Dean angrily.

"Maybe it's not all their fault," Dad said. "After all, cats don't know any better than to take fish when they see them in a pan. But you boys should have known better than to leave fish out like that. Why didn't you clean them and have Granny put them in the freezer as soon as you came back from the pond?"

Dean answered, "Well, when we got back it was supper time, so we couldn't do it right then."

"And we were tired after supper," Rickey added.

"I'm sure you were," said Dad. "But going fishing is like any other job. You need to finish it diligently or you may find you've wasted all the time you've put into it. Remember, Proverbs 12:27 says, 'The slothful man roasteth not that which he took in hunting.'"

Dean picked up the dish pan and sadly dumped the water out. "I guess that's true of fishing, too," he said.

Application questions

1. What would a slothful boy's bedroom look like?

2. How would a slothful girl go about her school work?

3. What would happen to a sluggard's paintbrushes? Tools? Toys? Books?

The Diligent Person

(Hard working, determined, persistent)

Proverbs 4:23

1. This verse tells us that we must be diligent to guard something. What is it? Why do you think it might be important to guard it diligently?

____

____

____

____

____

Proverbs 10:4

2. What happens to the person who works carelessly or lazily?

____

3. What happens to a person who works diligently? Why do you think this happens?

____

____

____

____

Proverbs 11:27

4. What comes to the man who is diligent in seeking good?

____

5. Favor is described as kindness from others or having others think well of us. Why would this happen if we are diligent in seeking good?

____

____

____

____

____

Proverbs 12:11

6. What happens to a man who works hard in his fields?

____

7. Do you think that happens to a person who wastes his time?

____

Proverbs 12:24

8. Is a hard worker likely to be made a boss over other workers? ______________________________________

Proverbs 13:4

9. Is a diligent man likely to get what his soul needs?

____

Proverbs13:11

10. What happens to the wealth of the man who works hard?

____

11. What happens to the wealth of the man who tries to get money by cheating?

____

Proverbs 14:23

12. What would you tell a person who always talks about getting money but never wants to work for it?

____

____

Proverbs 16:3

13. What should we do before we go to work on our plans?

____

Proverbs 16:26

14. What is one thing that makes people want to work diligently?

____

Proverbs 21:5

15. What happens when a man is diligent in planning his work?

____

Proverbs 22:29

16. When a person is diligent in his work, what kind of people want him to work for them?__________________

Proverbs 23:4

17. Some goals aren't worth working diligently for. What is one of them?

____

Proverbs 24:27

18. Is it wiser to work on building your house or your business first? Why do you think this might be true?

____

____

____

____

Proverbs 27:23

19. What are we to diligently know? Why might this be important?

____

____

____

Proverbs 28:19

20. What will the man have who works hard at growing things?

____

21. What will come to the man who wastes his time?

____

Proverbs 31:13

22. How does the excellent wife feel about working with her hands?

____

Proverbs 31:15

23. Does she get up early to start working? ____________

Proverbs 31:20

24. The diligent woman has the things she needs for her family, and some extra things also. What does she do with the extra things? ______________________________

Proverbs 31:24

25. What is something the diligent woman does to earn money for her family?

____

Proverbs 31:31

26. Do other people respect the diligence of the virtuous woman? ____________________________________

An Example of Diligence

"Do I have to eat my asparagus? David asked as the family sat at supper.

His father smiled. "I'm afraid you do, son. It's good for you."

David poked the green stalks with his fork. "I'll be glad when I'm grown up," he said. "Then I won't have to do things I don't like to do."

Dad smiled again. "That's funny, Dave. I was just thinking about something I had to do today that I didn't like."

"You mean you still have to do those things too, Dad? What was it?"

"Well, today I had to promote one of the men who work for me at the shop over another man who has worked for us much longer."

"Really? Why didn't you like that?" David wanted to know.

"Well, son, when a person has worked for me for many years, I like to see them move up in the company. I like to give them more pay and let them be leaders for the other workers. But today I had to choose between two men in shop, one who has been with me for five years and one who just started last year. I would have liked to give the boss job to Steve, because he has been with me longer. But I had to give it to the new man, Charles, instead."

"Why did you have to that?" David wondered.

"Because Charles is a hard worker and Steve isn't. Charles always gets to work early and Steve is often a few minutes late. Charles stays busy all day long, while Steve sometimes spends too much time talking with the other workers. Charles doesn't know as much about the job because he's only been with us for a year, but he gets a lot of work done because he's very diligent."

David was confused. "But if a person is getting a new job, one where he doesn't have to do as much work and mostly just tells other people what to do, what difference does it make whether he's a hard worker or not?"

His father finished his coffee and sat his cup down on the table. "That's a good question, son. The reason that the leader has to be a hard worker is this: if the other workers see a lazy man moved up to a higher job, they may feel that it doesn't matter whether a person works hard or not. They might figure that if their new boss doesn't have to work hard, then they shouldn't either. Most people work harder and better if their leader is diligent himself."

"You mean, he has to be a good example?" David asked.

"Exactly, Dave. The leader sets the pace for everybody. And that's why diligent people usually are leaders over lazy people. It's as the Bible says in Proverbs 12:24: 'The hand of the diligent shall bear rule: but the slothful shall be under tribute.'"

"What does it mean to be under tribute?"

"It means you have to stay at the bottom of the group and do the simple work. It means you have to be a follower instead of a leader. But people like Charles will always rise to the top because they're diligent."

Application questions

Talk about these questions with your parents.

1. List some things a diligent man would do to make his yard neat.

2. Name three people you know who show diligence.

3. What are three bad things that could happen in your home if no one was diligent?

Fun Quiz

Read the sentences below. If the sentence tells something about a diligent person, put an **X** under **DILIGENT** on that line. If the sentence tells something about a slothful person, put an **X** under **SLOTHFUL** on that line. Let's see how well you remember!

	DILIGENT	SLOTHFUL
1. He needs to learn from the ants.	________	________
2. He will increase in wealth.	________	________
3. He sleeps too much.	________	________
4. He causes trouble for those who send him to do things.	________	________
5. His plans work well.	________	________
6. He is the kind of person kings want to work for them.	________	________
7. He won't have enough to eat.	________	________
8. He carefully watches the condition of his flocks and herds.	________	________

	DILIGENT	SLOTHFUL
9. His fields are covered with thorns and nettles.	__________	__________
10. He won't plow when he should, so he will be begging at harvest.	__________	__________
11. She gets up early to start working.	__________	__________
12. He doesn't think about the future.	__________	__________
13. He has more than he needs, so he shares with others.	__________	__________
14. She is prepared for the coming of winter.	__________	__________
15. He makes up excuses to stay away from work.	__________	__________

Answers on page 21

The hand of the diligent shall bear rule.

Prov. 12:24

Answers to Fun Quiz:

1. Slothful
2. Diligent
3. Slothful
4. Slothful
5. Diligent
6. Diligent
7. Slothful
8. Diligent
9. Slothful
10. Slothful
11. Diligent
12. Slothful
13. Diligent
14. Diligent
15. Slothful

Look up the verses below and write answers to the questions.

The Righteous Man

(Right, just)

Proverbs 10:3

1. What does God promise the righteous man about food?

____

2. Do unrighteous people have this promise from God?

____

Proverbs 10:11

3. What is the difference between the words of the righteous man and the words of the wicked man?

____

____

Proverbs 10:24-28

4. Which kind of person will receive the desires of his heart? ____

5. Do you think a righteous man has much to fear? ______

6. Does a righteous man have a reason to be hopeful? (verse 28) ___________________________

7. What comes out of a righteous man's mouth?

____

Proverbs 11:8

8. What happens when a righteous man gets in trouble?

____

Proverbs 11:10

9. How do other people feel when things go well for the righteous? ___________________________

Proverbs 11:19

10. Does the way we live have anything to do with how long we live? ___________________________

Proverbs 11:21

11. Is there a blessing for the children of righteous people?

____

Proverbs 11:28-31

12. Which helps a man more, riches or righteousness? (verse 28)______________________________

13. What does God call the fruit of a righteous man? (verse 30) ______________________________

14. Do the rewards of righteousness start before we get to heaven? (verse 31) _________________________

Proverbs 12:5

15. What is the difference between the way a righteous man thinks and the way a wicked man thinks?

____

Proverbs 12:10

16. Is a righteous person kind to animals? __________

Proverbs 13:5

17. How does the righteous man feel about dishonesty?

____

Proverbs 13:25

18. Will the righteous man have enough to eat? _________

Proverbs 14:32

19. Is the righteous man afraid of dying? Why or why not?____

____

Proverbs 15:28-29

20. Which kind of person is more careful to speak good things? ____

21. What does righteous living do for our prayers?

____

Proverbs 18:10

22. Where do righteous people go for protection?

____

Proverbs 21:25,26

23. How do righteous people act toward people who need things? ______________________________

Proverbs 23:24,25

24. How can you make your parents happy?

____

Proverbs 24:15,16

25. What does a righteous man do when he runs into trouble?

____

____

Proverbs 25:26

26. What is it like when a righteous man fails to stand against wickedness?

____

____

Proverbs 28:1

27. Is a righteous man brave? _______________ How about a wicked man? _______________

Proverbs 28:12

28. What happens when righteous people triumph?

____

29. What happens when wicked people rise in power?

____

Proverbs 29:6

30. Does a righteous man get trapped in sin? ___________

Proverbs 29:7

31. Does the righteous man care about the rights of poor people? _______________________________________

An Example of Righteousness

Nine-year-old Libbie hung on tightly to her father's hand as he led her through the biggest crowd she had ever seen.

"Are we almost there, Daddy?" she asked.

Her father answered, "One more block, honey. And it looks like we're just about on time, too. Nobody's on the platform yet, but there's quite a lot of people gathered around it already."

They were hurrying to the park in the middle of town to see the mayor present an important gift to Sam Tracy, a man who lived just a few houses down the street from their home. It seemed to Libbie that the whole town was gathering as people streamed toward the park from every direction. It was as if a circus had come to town.

Her father had said that Sam Tracy didn't have an enemy in the world. As far back as any one could remember, he had been doing kind things for people and helping anybody in need. He had always been available to mow the lawn of a sick neighbor, help out with a home repair project, or give a few dollars from his limited funds to a good cause.

"Daddy, why are so many people here?" Libbie asked as they crossed the parking lot and started walking over the grass. "Are they all here to see Mr. Tracy?"

Her father began to slow down as they approached the edge of the crowd around the platform. "Yes, Libbie, we're all here to honor Sam. And it's shaping up to be quite a celebration, too." He looked around at the rapidly growing group of people. They were milling around, chatting with friends and neighbors in the Saturday morning sunshine while hot dog vendors distributed snacks and drinks as fast as they could work.

"Are we celebrating because he got out of the hospital?"

"Well, yes," her father answered. "And we're also celebrating what he did for little Danny. He almost died because of it, you know."

Libbie did know. Daddy had read to her from the newspaper the story of how old Mr. Tracy had been taking his daily walk around town when he had seen smoke coming from the Norton's house. Mrs. Norton had been working in her flower bed in the side yard while her two-year-old son Danny had been taking his nap upstairs. Somehow a fire had started in the attic and Mr. Tracy had seen smoke coming from an upstairs window as he walked by.

Some of the neighbors had seen what happened then. They said Mr. Tracy had shouted to Mrs. Norton that her house was on fire and she had come running around to the front sidewalk. Of course she had been terrified because Danny was in the house alone. She had tried to run up the steps and into the house for him, but Mr. Tracy had held her back and said he would go instead. He had asked which room Danny was in and told her to stand underneath Danny's window. Then he had run into the house and climbed the stairs to the second floor, where smoke was rapidly filling the rooms as little tongues of flame began to lick at the attic windows overhead. He had found little Danny sleeping peacefully in his bed. Because the bedroom door had been closed, the smoke had not hurt him. The little boy must have been surprised when Mr. Tracy had snatched him up, wrapped him in his bedsheet and dropped him out the window into the arms of his mother a few feet below.

But it had been harder to get out of the house than to get in. The upstairs had been full of blinding, choking smoke as Mr. Tracy ran down the hallway to the stairwell. He had made it to the stairs, coughing and gasping, but had fallen and broken his hip as he tried to make his way down. The firemen had arrived just in time to carry him down the rest of the steps and out into the fresh air.

That had happened weeks ago, and Mr. Tracy had just been out of the hospital a few days. Now the town had arranged this special celebration for him.

"Here they come!" Libbie's father said. He hoisted her to his shoulders as a white car with no top on it drove up to the platform. She recognized Mr. Tracy and the town mayor in the back seat. Mr. Tracy was helped up the steps of the platform where the Mayor made a short speech and then pinned a medal on his shirt. The crowd went wild, clapping and cheering.

Later, as they walked home, Libbie looked up at her father. "Daddy," she said.

"Yes, Lib?"

"I'm glad we had a special day for Mr. Tracy. He's a good man, isn't he?"

"Yes, honey, he really is. Always doing something for somebody else. Always trying to do what's right."

"I'm glad we gave him that medal. And I'm glad so many people came to celebrate his getting well and coming home from the hospital. It looked like the whole town was there."

Her dad stopped suddenly and looked down at her, smiling. "You know, Libbie, there's a good Bible lesson in this. Do you remember we were reading in Proverbs last night?"

"Yes, Daddy."

"Well, one verse we read really sticks in my mind because of Mr. Tracy today. It's Proverbs 11:10. It says, "When it goeth well with the righteous, the city rejoiceth."

Libbie thought about that as they started walking again. Yes, that was what they were doing today. The whole city was rejoicing for Mr. Tracy.

Application Questions

Talk about these questions with your mother or father.

1. What do you think are some reasons that other people rejoice when the righteous do well?

2. Proverbs 11:21 says that the children of the righteous will have special protection. What do you think this means? From what kind of things might they be delivered?

3. A righteous man is concerned about the life of his animals. What things do you think a righteous man might do for his dog before leaving on vacation?

The Wicked Man

(Wrong, ungodly)

Proverbs 2:22

1. Do wicked people have a bright future? Why or why not?

____

____

Proverbs 3:25,26

2. Will good people be caught up in God's judgment on the wicked? _______________________________________

Proverbs 3:33

3. Should wicked people expect God to bless their homes?

____

Proverbs 4:14-19

4. Should you spend a lot of time with wicked people? (verses 14, 15) ________________

5. Do wicked people want to help or hurt others? (verse 17) ______________________________

6. Do wicked people understand why their problems come? (verse 19) ___________________

Proverbs 5:21-23

7. Does God notice what the wicked are doing? (verse21)

____

8. What causes the wicked to be tied up in problems? (verse 22) ____

9. Does the wicked man listen to instruction? (verse 23)____________________________

10. What happens to him because of this? (verse 23)

____

Proverbs 9:7-9

11. Does a wicked man like those who try to give him good counsel? _____________________

Proverbs 10:6

12. Does the wicked man speak kindly? ________________

Proverbs 10:7

13. Does the wicked man leave good memories for others when he dies? ______________________________________

Proverbs 10:24,25

14. Does the wicked man have a reason to be afraid of the future? _________________________________

Proverbs 10:27

15. Should the wicked man expect a long life? __________

Proverbs 11:7

16. Does the wicked man have a reason to fear dying?

____

Proverbs 11:17

17. Is it good for a city to have wicked people in it?

____

Proverbs 11:18

18. Does a wicked man do honest works? _____________

Proverbs 12:6

19. Can you tell a man is wicked by his words? _________

Proverbs 12:7

20. Can a wicked man expect to have a long and successful life? ______________________

Proverbs 12:12

21. Does the wicked man hope to profit from doing evil?

____

Proverbs 12:26

22. What happens to those who follow the example of the wicked man? ____________

Proverbs 13:17

23. What happens when a wicked man is trusted to carry messages?

____

____

Proverbs 14:19

24. Who will end up ruling over the wicked?

____

Proverbs 15:8

25. What does the Lord think of sacrifices offered to Him by wicked people?

____

____

Proverbs 15:9

26. How does God feel about the way a wicked man lives?

____

____

Proverbs 16:4

27. Does the Lord have a use for wicked people? _______

Proverbs 17:15

28. Should others make excuses for the wicked man?

____

Proverbs 17:23

29. Would a wicked man make a good judge? Why or why not?

____

____

Proverbs 18:3

30. Does the wicked man get respect from others?

____

Proverbs 19:28

31. Should the words of a wicked man be trusted in court? Why or why not?

____

____

____

Proverbs 20:26

32. Should a ruler allow wicked people around?

____

Proverbs 21:4

33. Is a wicked person proud or humble?

____

Proverbs 21:7

34. What is the wicked man's attitude toward justice?

____

____

Proverbs 21:10

35. How does the wicked man feel about others around him?

____

____

Proverbs 21:27

36. Is it bad for a wicked person to bring a sacrifice to God? What can make it even worse?

____

____

Proverbs 21:29

37. Does a wicked man act humble toward others?

____

Proverbs 24:19, 20

38. How should you feel about a wicked man when he seems to be doing very well right now?

____

____

Proverbs 24:24,25

39. How will others feel about you if you say that wicked people are doing right?

40. How will they treat you if you rebuke wickedness?

Proverbs 25:4,5

41. Why is it wise for a ruler to stay away from the wicked?

Proverbs 28:4

42. What kind of people think that the wicked are good?

Proverbs 28:15

43. What is it like when a wicked ruler is over poor people?

____

____

Proverbs 29:2

44. How do people feel when a wicked ruler is over them?____

Proverbs 29:12

45. If a king sets a wicked example, what happens to his helpers?

____

____

Proverbs 29:16

46. What happens when there are a lot of wicked people around?

____

____

Proverbs 29:27

47. How do wicked men and righteous men feel about each other?

___

___

___

An Example of Wickedness

Libbie was sitting on her father's lap as he read to her from the Bible.

"Proverbs 28:1," he started. "The wicked flee when no man pursueth: but the righteous are bold as a lion."

He started to read the next verse but Libbie stopped him with a question, as she often did.

"Daddy, what does that mean? The part about the wicked man?"

Daddy thought a minute. "Well, I think it means that when a person lives a wicked life, they have a lot to worry about. If you do a lot of things that are wrong, God will spank you for it sooner or later. And of course there are a lot of things a wicked person has to fear from other people, too."

"Like what kind of things?" Libbie asked.

"Well, I expect a lot of things. I remember a boy who grew up in my neighborhood who lived a wicked life, and though he did most of his mischief to have fun, there wasn't much fun to it. He made a lot of people angry at him and he stayed in trouble most of the time. His name was Bill and he was a couple of years older than I was. Nobody liked him much, I don't think."

"Because he was wicked?"

"That's right. And he was a good example of fleeing when no one's pursuing. Once he threw a rock at a dog and hurt it. Then he found out that the dog belonged to the biggest, toughest boy in the neighborhood. He was so scared when he heard that the boy had found out about it that everywhere he went, he was constantly looking around for that boy. Even when he was nowhere around, Bill had to be on the lookout for him."

"So he was afraid even when he didn't have to be?"

"Yep. And it went on that way for years. He stole some bubble gum from the store down the street and got caught, so he was afraid to go back in that store any more. Later on, as a teenager, he started stealing things like bicycles and tools out of garages. He sold some of those things but the money didn't do him any good. All the time, he was looking over his shoulder for fear of being found out.

"When Bill was a young man he went to jail for selling drugs. When he got out he came back to the neighborhood where we lived. As long as I knew him, he was always fearful and suspicious. He was always very nervous when a policeman was around."

"Even if the policeman wasn't after him?" Libbie asked.

"Yes, even then."

Libby was thoughtful. "That wouldn't be much fun. I'd hate to be scared all the time when there was nothing to be scared of."

"No," said Daddy. "A person may get a few dollars by doing wicked things, but it ruins their life. 'The wicked flee when no man pursueth.'"

Application Questions

Talk about these questions with your mother or father.

1. Proverbs 10:7 says that the memory of the righteous will be blessed while the name of the wicked shall rot. Can you think of any people in history or in the Bible who were so wicked that people still talk badly about them today?

2. The Bible says that it is bad for wicked people to rule over others. What problems might it cause if they did?

3. A wicked man doesn't like righteous people. Why might that be?

Fun Quiz

Read the sentences below. If the sentence tells something about a righteous person, put an **X** under **RIGHTEOUS** on that line. If the sentence tells something about a wicked person, put an **X** under **WICKED** on that line. Let's see how well you remember!

	RIGHTEOUS	WICKED
1. He will always have food.	________	________
2. He flees when no one is chasing him.	________	________
3. He will live longer because of the way he lives.	________	________
4. He makes trouble for himself all his life.	________	________
5. He gets trapped by his own sin.	________	________
6. He cares about poor people.	________	________
7. He doesn't understand why he has troubles.	________	________

	RIGHTEOUS	WICKED
8. He won't listen to good counsel.	____________	____________
9. He isn't afraid of dying.	____________	____________
10. He hopes to gain money by doing evil.	____________	____________
11. What he has is better than riches.	____________	____________
12. He can't stand dishonest dealing.	____________	____________
13. He is proud.	____________	____________
14. The name of the Lord is his strong tower.	____________	____________

Answers on page 49

The righteous are bold as a lion.

Prov. 28:1b

Quiz Answers:

1. Righteous
2. Wicked
3. Righteous
4. Wicked
5. Wicked
6. Righteous
7. Wicked
8. Wicked
9. Righteous
10. Wicked
11. Righteous
12. Righteous
13. Wicked
14. Righteous

Look up the verses below and write answers to the questions

The Self-confident Fool

(Hebrew, *kesil*)

Proverbs 1:22

1. Does this fool appreciate knowledge?

____

Proverbs 1:32

2. What will destroy this fool?

____

Proverbs 3:35

3. What will this fool inherit?

____

Proverbs 8:5

4. What is wisdom crying out to this fool.?

____

Proverbs 10:18

5. Does the self-confident fool talk badly about others?

____

____

Proverbs 10:23

6. How does this fool have fun?

____

Proverbs 12:23

7. Does this fool like to talk? What does he speak about?

____

Proverbs 13:16

8. Do others know he is a fool? If so, how do they know?

____

____

Proverbs 13:19

9. What is an abomination to this fool?

____

Proverbs 13:20

10. What will happen to the one who walks with or spends much time with this type of fool?

____

Proverbs 14:8

11. The prudent man realizes that there are consequences to acting a certain way. Does the fool? Who does he deceive?

____

____

Proverbs 14:16

12. Is this fool unsure of himself?____________________

Proverbs 14:24

13. What does this fool sow and reap?

____

____

Proverbs 14:33

14. Does this fool often keep his thoughts to himself, or does he blurt out all he knows?

____

Proverbs 15:14

15. The prudent seek knowledge. What does the "kesil" seek?____________________________________

Proverbs 17:10

16. A wise man learns from reproof. Does the kesil fool learn easily? What does he learn from?

____

____

Proverbs 17:12

17. What character trait of a fool do you think this verse is talking about? ______________________________

Proverbs 17:16

18. How does a fool try to get wisdom?

____

19. Is his heart prepared to receive wisdom? ___________

Proverbs 17:21

20. How does this fool's father feel?

____

Proverbs 17:24

21. Where are the fool's eyes? Is he a contented person?

____

____

Proverbs 18:2

22. Does this fool try to learn from others by talking to them, or just to tell them what he thinks?

____

Proverbs 18:6

23. Is this fool eager to make peace? _____________

Proverbs 18:7

24. What is his destruction? What is a snare to his soul?

____

Proverbs 19:1

25. What is a "kesil's" speech like?

____

Proverbs 19:10

26. What would be bad for this fool?

____

Proverbs 19:29

27. What will get through to a fool? What is prepared for him? ______________________________________

____

Proverbs 23:9

28. Should you share your wisdom with a fool?
If you did, what would he do?

____

Proverbs 26:1

29. Luxury, we learned, is not fitting for a fool. What else is not fitting for this fool?______________________________

Proverbs 26:3

30. Will this fool do what he is told, on his own?

____

Proverbs 26:4,5

31. How should you answer a fool? Why?

____

____

____

Proverbs 26:6

32. Should you send this fool to deliver a message for you?

____

33. Who will be harmed if you send a message with a fool?

____

____

____

Proverbs 26:7

34. Do fools understand proverbs?__________ Can they communicate them to others?_________________________

Proverbs 26:7,9

35. What two things are a proverb in the mouth of a fool compared to?

____

____

Proverbs 26:8

36. Should one give honor to a fool?_____________ If he does, what is he compared to? _______________________

____

Proverbs 26:10

37. Should an employer hire a kesil fool?______________

Proverbs 26:11

38. Does a fool repeat his folly? What is he like?

____

Proverbs 26:12

39. What type of man has even less hope than a kesil fool ?

____

____

Proverbs 29:20

40. What is another kind of man who has less hope?

____

Proverbs 28:26

41. What does this fool trust in? ____________________

____

Proverbs 29:11

42. Does a fool control his words? _________________

An Example of a Self-Confident Fool

Eight-year-old Henrietta Faulkner was visiting her relatives in Virginia in the spring of 1846. Her cousin Alicia was the same age, but the girls had different interests.

Henrietta liked daring games, such as climbing the maple trees higher than the boys did. Alicia was very ladylike, and couldn't bear to get her clothes torn or messy. So, sometimes they didn't get along very well together, and such was the case today.

It started out in the morning. It was the first day of July, and the last day Henrietta would be on the farm. Her mother was going to come for her that afternoon to take her back home to the city. She had seen Alicia's brother Andrew walking on the top railing of the pigpen fence, and she was talking about it to Alicia.

"It would be lots of fun," she told her cousin. "Wouldn't it? Think of how ashamed the boys would be of themselves to see me walk it without falling, and to do it in less time than they can."

Alicia looked up from buttoning her shoes. "That wouldn't be safe, Hettie," she replied. "You would probably fall in. Have you ever walked on a rail?"

"N-no, but I'm sure I could," Henrietta laughed. "It doesn't look hard at all. I walked out on the limb of that big oak tree above the pond. Remember that?"

"Yes, I do. When you took the second step, you fell and hung there by the lace on your dress. You stayed there in the tree until Andrew and Papa climbed up there to release you. You'll end up in a mess, Hettie, I promise you."

Henrietta laughed. "Well, I'm going downstairs to eat breakfast."

"And then you're going outside, aren't you?"

"I might." Hettie skipped out of the room and slid down the banister, landing on a heap on the floor below.

"Ouch!" she thought. *"I hope Alicia didn't see that!"*

No one had seen the little mishap, so she went to the dining room where the maid, Miranda, was setting the table for breakfast. "Hello, Miranda," Henrietta greeted her. "What's for breakfast?"

"Oh, de usual," Miranda replied, smiling. "Oatmeal, pancakes and sausage. And what are you plannin' on doin' today, Miz Hettie?"

Henrietta smiled. "Oh, nothing much," she replied cautiously. Changing the subject, she asked, "Where's Aunt Lucinda?"

"She's comin' right down, chile. She'll be in here for breakfast soon."

Alicia came into the dining room. As soon as Miranda left the room, she warned her cousin again, "Hettie, you're going to break your neck and you won't be able to go home for six months!"

Henrietta laughed. "Oh, Alicia, you're so worrisome! I can do it; I'm not a sissy. Just watch. You'll see!" she promised.

Mrs. Hopkins came downstairs just then and joined them. "As soon as Andrew and Adam come downstairs, we'll be ready to eat," she said.

Mr. Hopkins and Andrew came in just as she said it, and when every one was seated, the blessing was asked and breakfast began.

As soon as she had finished the last bite, Henrietta drained her cup and asked to be excused. Alicia had hardly eaten a bite.

"Hurry up," Henrietta hissed. Alicia excused herself and followed her cousin.

"You're not really going to try it, are you?" she asked. "You wouldn't dare, would you?"

"See if I don't!" Henrietta laughed as they reached the pigsty.

"Hettie, please don't! You're not being reasonable!" Alicia pleaded.

"Phew! It sure smells bad!" her cousin commented, wrinkling her nose, as she put her foot on the bottom rail of the fence.

"Hettie, I'm going to tell Mother!"

Henrietta looked disgustedly at her cousin. "Alicia, don't be such a baby! I can do it! Just watch." She stepped out on the fence. She kept her balance! Delightedly, she began to run. "See, Alicia! What did I tell you?"

But the other girl had already run for the house as fast as her feet could carry her.

"Oh, shucks." Henrietta was still running. Uh-oh! She was coming close to the end of the fence.

"Hettie! Hettie Faulkner! Stop, oh, do stop!" her aunt called frantically. "You'll get hurt!"

Henrietta laughed. Just then, though, she lost her footing and slipped down into the soft, gooey mud. "Aaaaaah!" she screamed, as the mud oozed into her shoes. She felt herself sinking.

But her aunt pulled her out, just before a big hog reached her. Over the fence, missing a shoe, a necklace, and two gold bracelets her uncle had just given her.

"Oh, Hettie!" Mrs. Hopkins sighed. "Your mother came early to pick you up, and here you were in your new dress she sent only a week ago!"

Mrs. Faulkner wasn't very pleased with her daughter. "Henrietta! Do you know how much I paid for that dress? And your uncle gave you that jewelry recently, Andrew told me."

"Alicia warned her not to do it," Andrew told Aunt Judith. "I heard them talking about it when I went to feed the cats in the barn and when they were in their bedroom."

As she was changing her clothes, Henrietta paused to look at the open Bible on the vanity. It was opened to Proverbs, and the twenty-sixth verse of chapter 23 seemed to jump out at her: "He that trusteth in his own heart is a fool; but whoso walketh wisely, he shall be delivered."

"That Alicia," Henrietta grumbled to herself. "I'll bet she opened it to that verse on purpose."

But she knew that Alicia had warned her. If she hadn't been self-confident, and if she had listened to her cousin, she could have avoided all the trouble.

Look up the verses below and write answers to the questions.

The Stubborn Fool

(Hebrew *evil*)

Proverbs 1:7

1. How do these fools feel about wisdom and instruction?

____

____

2. Does this type of fool fear God? ________________

Proverbs 7:22

3. Does this fool naturally choose right or wrong? Does he realize what the consequence will be to his choice?

____

____

Proverbs 10:8,10

4. Webster's Dictionary defines "prating" as continued talk, or talking too much about idle, or useless subjects. What will happen to a prating fool?______________________

____

Proverbs 10:21

5. Does a fool have wisdom to share with others? Would he make a good counselor?

____

____

Proverbs 11:29

6. How does a fool affect his family?

____

7. What will a fool inherit? ______________________________

____

8. Will this type of fool be a leader or a servant? Whom will he lead or serve? ___________________________________

____

____

Proverbs 12:15

9. Does this type of fool realize his need for help?

____

10. Will he go to a wise man for counsel?

____

Proverbs 12:16

11. Does he have a temper? ____________________

12. Will he be able to hide his temper from others?

____

Proverbs 15:5

13. Does he listen to his father's instruction? __________

Proverbs 16:22

14. What kind of counsel would this fool give?

____

Proverbs 20:3

15. Does a fool mind his own business? ____________

16. Does he cause strife? ____________________

Proverbs 24:7

17. Would this fool be comfortable around wise people?

____

Prov. 27:22

18. Is this type of fool quick to turn from his ways when he meets up with harsh reproofs?________________________

An Example of a Stubborn Fool

Samuel Snyder was one of those boys who gets a nickname from the way he acts. Stubborn Sam was his. He was always getting in trouble because he was so stubborn.

Once his mother had told him to wait till she could get there to drain the noodles. Instead, he took the lid off himself, steam-burning his arm as he did so.

You'd think Stubborn Sam would eventually learn to stop being stubborn, wouldn't you? Well, he didn't. He was too stubborn to learn! That is how he got in trouble on July the second.

Sam's sister Stacy had come home from school excitedly a week before, announcing that Mr. Overton was conducting a school fair. There was going to be a big surprise award for the one who could make the best science model, and Doug Hilton was trying for the prize. All the boys were sure he would win. So Sam stubbornly decided to show them that old Doug wouldn't get the prize he was so desperate to have.

"I'm going to make this model of a skeleton," he decided. "It shows how the bones work, and you're supposed to use batteries so they really move. I'll make a poster to go with it. Isn't that neat?" He demonstrated to Stacy how everything would work.

"Can I help Sammy?" little Stephen asked.

"No, Stevie! You'd mess it up terribly!" Samuel shouted. "Keep your hands away from my model!"

"Oh, Sam, be nice," Stacy scolded him. "Come, Stevie, you can watch Salina and me make our dolls for the hobby exhibition."

Sam was glad Stacy took the three-year old away. He got to work on his project.

"Mom," he called a little later, "where do I attach this piece?"

"I don't know, Sam," his mother replied, a moment later, as she looked at it carefully. "I'm not very good with projects like this one. You'd better wait till your dad gets home. "

"That'll be at least another hour!" Sam protested loudly.

He took the plastic hammer that the box included and went to work, never minding the directions. Soon every single bone was broken.

So he tried another project, hanging the planets in space. That one messed up, too, because he didn't learn from his mistakes.

Stacy and Salina finished their doll exhibit that night, and the next day took it over to the school.

On the night of the fair, Sam had no model. He'd worked on four different ones and ruined them all because he was too stubborn to wait for help.

Stacy pointed to a model that had been done carelessly. "Look, Sam," she said, "it's Doug's. He won the first prize."

"For *that* ugly thing?" Samuel squealed. "That's ridiculous."

His mother nodded. "Yes, it is. If you had only learned the first time, and quit being stubborn, you'd have that blue ribbon, and probably some money besides."

Sam looked sadly at Doug Hilton's model.

But guess what? The next year the same thing happened. Other people would sometimes win the blue ribbon, besides Doug, but Stubborn Sam was none of those people, though he tried another project every single year.

Though thou shouldest bray a fool in a mortal among wheat with a pestle, yet will not his foolishness depart from him.

Proverbs 27:22

Look up the verses below and answer the questions.

The Simple Fool

(Hebrew *pethi*)

Proverbs 1:4

1. Were the Proverbs written specially for the simple fool among others? ___________ Can the simple man learn wisdom? ___________

Proverbs 1:22

2. Does the simple man choose to be simple? Does he enjoy it?______________________________________

Proverbs 1:32

3. What will happen to the simple if he decides to continue in his folly? ____________________________________

____

Proverbs 7:7,8

4. What kind of man is tricked by a strange woman?

____

Proverbs 8:1-5

5. Is wisdom calling out to the simple person?

____

Proverbs 9:4-6

6. What must the simple do before he can acquire understanding?________________________________

____

Proverbs 9:13-18

7. Should a simple man listen to a foolish woman? Why or why not?____________________________________

____

____

Proverbs 14:15

8. Is the simple man is quick to believe what others tell him?____

Proverbs 14:18

9. What happens to the person who continues to be a simple fool?

____

Proverbs 19:25

10. What will get the attention of the simple fool and cause him to learn?

____

____

Proverbs 22:3 & 27:12

11. Does the simple realize that there are problems ahead and prepare for them?______________________________

An Example of a Simple Fool

Danny and Roger were two boys who lived on the same street. They had been friends for a long time and did many things together. Danny was a little older than Roger, so he was the leader and Roger usually did whatever Danny wanted to do.

One day the two boys were walking down the street when they passed a high fence made of boards.

"I wonder what's on the other side?" said Roger.

"I think I'll find out," Danny said. And he jumped up to grab the top of the fence, then started scrambling to bring his whole body up.

"Danny, you'd better not. There's a 'DANGER:KEEP OUT' sign over here." Roger was nervous. But Danny never paid much attention to rules. Now he scoffed at Roger's warning.

"Aw, who cares?" he demanded scornfully. "There's nobody around. Hey, look at this. They're building a house back here!"

Roger looked up and down the fence, but the boards were so close together that he had to walk some distance before he found a crack he could see through. Meanwhile, Danny had jumped down on the other side of the fence and was walking around looking at the construction machines. Seeing a tractor, he climbed up onto the seat. Roger's heart thudded as his friend started the tractor and began to drive it slowly across the grassy vacant lot.

"Danny! Stop that tractor and get back out of here, quick! You'll be in big trouble!" Roger yelled. But Danny just grinned and began to drive in circles.

"Don't worry, this is easy," he called back. "I always drive the tractors on Uncle Jim's farm. Come on over and try it!"

It did look easy. And it looked like fun. Roger was still nervous, but Danny was having such a good time that he was tempted to climb the fence himself and take a turn on the tractor. Roger stood with his eye to the crack in the fence, wondering whether he should try it.

Just at that moment, Danny drove over a board lying in the grass. He expected to hear it crackle as it broke under the tractor's weight, but instead heard a pop and a long hiss as the air began to escape from one of the tractor's big rear tires.

"Oh no! That board had a nail in it!" Danny yelled. Hurriedly he turned off the engine, jumped off the tractor and climbed back over the fence. The two boys ran away at top speed and didn't stop; until they were out of sight in the woods at the edge of town. Then they separated and went to their homes.

A few days later, Roger was telling his dad about what had happened.

"I've already heard about that," his father said. "Somebody saw Danny in there and his dad gave him a whipping and made him pay for fixing the tractor. I'm sure glad you didn't climb that fence, too."

"So am I," Roger said solemnly. "Danny looked like he was having such a good time on that tractor that I was almost tempted to try it too. But after hearing what happened to him, I'll never go where I'm not supposed to."

"That's a wise decision, son," Dad replied. "You're young and there's a lot you don't know about life, but this time you got to learn a lesson at some one else's expense."

Smite a scorner and the simple will beware...
Proverbs 19:25a

Look up the verses below and answer the questions.

The Scorning Fool

(Hebrew *lutz*)

Webster's Dictionary: *A scorner is one who scoffs at religion, its ordinances, teachers and who makes a mock of sin, and the judgements and threatenings of God against sinners.*

Proverbs 1:22

1. God says we should delight ourselves in Him. What do scorners delight themselves in? ______________________

____

Proverbs 3:34

2. God gives grace (desire and power to do His will) to the humble. How does God treat scorners?________________

____

Proverbs 9:7

3. Should we try to correct a scorner? _____ Why or why not? ______________________________________

____

Proverbs 13:1

4. Does a scorner obey his father? __________

Proverbs 14:6

5. Does a scorner seek wisdom? Does he find wisdom?

____

Proverbs 15:12

6. Will a scorner go to a wise man for counsel?

____

Proverbs 15:12

7. How does a scorner feel about one who reproves him?

____

Proverbs 19:25 & 21:11

8. To give understanding to the simple, how should a scorner be dealt with? ____________________________

____

____

Proverbs 19:29

9. How does God deal with a scorner? ____________________

____

____

Proverbs 21:24

10. What are three character traits of a scorner found in this verse? ____

____

____

Proverbs 22:10

11. What does a scorner cause in a group of people? (Proverbs 22:10)

____

12. What should a group of people do to a scorner in their midst?____

____

Proverbs 24:9

13. God tells us to let our minds dwell on pure, true, lovely, honorable, virtuous things. What does a scorner think about? ______________________________

Proverbs 24:9

14. How do men view a scorner? ____________________

____

Proverbs 29:8

15. What effect do scornful men have on a city?

____

Proverbs 9:12

16. How will a scorner end up?____________________

____

Proverbs 19:28

17. Does a scorner rightly defend justice? Would he make a good witness in court?

____

An Example of a Scorning Fool

Horace Simpson answered the phone.

"Hello."

"Hi, Horace, let's go down to the rink and skate a while."

"Sure, Billy, why not?"

"When can you come?"

Horace glanced at the clock. "Edith told me to stay here till she gets home. She went grocery shopping and left me here with the kids, but they're sleeping now. She should be back pretty soon, so I guess I'll have to wait."

"Oh, I wouldn't want you to leave them while they're asleep, anyway. Well, I'll come over and by the time I get there, maybe she'll be back, OK?"

"OK."

As he hung up, Horace decided to see what there was to eat. Edith had told him not to eat any of the ham, but he didn't care. He made himself a huge ham sandwich, and then when Billy got there, he took his skates out and tried them out on the living room floor. Edith had told him not to, but he didn't care.

When she got home, she scolded him for breaking both of the rules. (She'd taken her orphan brother in when his parents died, and now she was a poor widow herself.) Horace just laughed at her. "Aw, those are stupid rules anyway. Why can't I skate in the house? Anyway, Billy and I are going to the rink. See you at suppertime."

"Don't be late," his sister called after him.

Horace scoffed, "I can be late if I want to. You're not my mom." She probably didn't hear him, but he didn't care about that, either.

"Hey, Horace, you ought to be more respectful to your sister," Billy suggested, as they crossed the street.

"No, thanks. She's my sister, as you just pointed out. Besides, she's silly anyway. Why can't I eat any ham? Does she want me to starve...? Hey, where are you going?"

"I should be asking *you* that."

"I'm crossing through the vacant lot. Nice shortcut, huh?"

"Great, except that there's a 'no trespassing' sign on that tree over there."

Horace laughed. "Gee, Billy, you're so scared of getting in trouble! Sure, I've gotten into my share of scrapes, but never in one that I couldn't get out of. Have some gum?"

"Sure."

They had just reached the park. Horace gave Billy a stick of gum and unwrapped one for himself, throwing the wrapper on the grass.

"Hey! Don't you see that sign over there?" Billy exclaimed. "You shouldn't be littering, Horace."

Horace sneered, "You're a scaredy-cat, aren't you? Billy's scared, Billy's scared!"

"At least I obey the rules," Billy remarked, a bit offended.

"Ha! I never did and never will, unless they're sensible. Well, we're close to the rink now. Let's cut through here."

"No, Horace! That's private property, too!"

"Humph! What do I care? Come on, you baby. Or are you afraid the skating rink's private property too?" Horace said scornfully.

* * * * *

"Billy, did you see this?"

Billy Thornton looked up from the book he was reading.

"What is it, Deborah?" he asked his wife.

"Remember your old friend, Horace, and how he always broke the rules long ago?"

Billy braced himself for what was coming. "Ah... sure, I, um... remember... uh, has anything happened to him?"

"Sure has! He kept on and on breaking rules of every kind, and now he's gotten in trouble with the law and serving a ten-year sentence in prison."

Billy sighed and returned to reading the chapter and verse he was on, Proverbs 19:29: *Judgments are prepared for scorners, and stripes for the back of fools* "So Horace's scorn has ended in judgment at last," he thought.

Look up the verses below and write answers to the questions.

NABAL FOOL

(Empty person, committed)

Proverbs 17:7

1. What kind of speech does a fool use?

____

Proverbs 17:21

2. How does the father of a nabal fool feel?

____

3. Is the father of a nabal fool glad he was born?__________

Proverbs 30:21-22

4. What concerning a fool makes even the earth quake?

____

Proverbs 30:22

5. Should we have anything to do with this kind of fool? _______________ What was the outcome of Nabal's life like?

____

Psalm 14:1

6. What has the fool said in his heart? _______________

____

Ezekiel 13:3

7. What does he often pretend to be? _______________

Psalm 74:18

8. What does he do to the Name of God?

____

9. Does he do this often? _______________

An Example of the Wicked Fool

The true story of a *nabal* fool is told in I Samuel chapter 25. In fact, this man's name was Nabal. The story took place when David, whom God had chosen to be king, was hiding with his friends in the wilderness from Saul, who was king at the time and who wanted to kill David so that David could never take the throne.

Nabal was a very rich man who had thousands of sheep and goats. A group of his helpers had been taking care of a herd of his sheep near where David and his men were staying. David's men had protected Nabal's helpers and the sheep. They had kept them safe from robbers and wild animals so that not one of Nabal's possessions had been lost during the weeks or months they had been near David.

When the time came for the sheep to be shorn so their wool could be sold, the many different flocks were gathered together in one place by Nabal's men. Shearing time was a time of hard work but also a time of celebration. Great feasts would be prepared for the workers during these days.

David sent some of his men to ask Nabal to share the feast with David's men, since they had guarded Nabal's workers and property and not charged him any money for doing so. But Nabal would not share. He had much wealth, but he was selfish and unkind, and didn't care that David's men had been living a hard life in the wilderness for a long time and had helped his own workers.

When the messengers returned to David and told them that Nabal had refused his request and treated them scornfully, he decided that wicked Nabal should be killed. He set out with 400 of his men to punish Nabal, but never got there.

One of Nabal's men went to Nabal's wife Abigail and told her what David was planning to do. He knew it would do no good to try to talk to Nabal and get him to change his mind about helping David. Nabal was too wicked to listen to anyone. So Abigail took a gift of food to David for him and his men. She met him just as he was coming to attack Nabal and because of her kindness, David changed his mind and decided to leave her husband alone.

The next morning Abigail told Nabal what she had done. Nabal was very frightened. Perhaps it was because he had come so close to being killed, or perhaps he was terrified that King Saul would find out that Nabal's wife had helped David, whom the king hated. His heart became like a stone in his chest. Ten days later, he died.

The Bible doesn't tell us about anyone who was sorry Nabal died. He was harsh and proud, selfish and did not fear God. David and his men, Nabal's own helpers and even his wife all knew that Nabal had been a wicked man and a fool.

Application Questions

1. Can you think of a way someone might get into trouble by being too self-confident?

2. Give an example of how stubborn fool might show that he is stubborn.

3. What are some ways a wise person could help a simple fool to do things better?

4. A scorning fool has no respect for the laws of God. How do you think this type of person would respond to other laws, such as the laws about driving a car?

5. The wicked fool says there is no God. Why do you think he might want to believe that?

Fun Quiz

	Simple	***Scornful***	***Stubborn***	***Self-Confident***	***Wicked***
1. He believes what he's told.	_____	_____	_____	_____	_____
2. He won't listen to reproof.	_____	_____	_____	_____	_____
3. Described as a "prating fool".	_____	_____	_____	_____	_____
4. He doesn't prepare ahead for trouble.	_____	_____	_____	_____	_____
5. It's hard to separate him from his foolishness.	_____	_____	_____	_____	_____
6. Smite him and the simple will beware.	_____	_____	_____	_____	_____
7. He trusts in his own heart.	_____	_____	_____	_____	_____
8. He learns by seeing others punished.	_____	_____	_____	_____	_____
9. Says there is no God to judge wickedness	_____	_____	_____	_____	_____
10. Mocks and despises parents' teachings.	_____	_____	_____	_____	_____

Answers:

1. Simple
2. Self-confident
3. Stubborn
4. Simple
5. Stubborn
6. Scornful
7. Self-confident
8. Simple
9. Wicked
10. Scornful

Look up the verses below and write answers to the questions.

The Prudent Man

Prudent: Wise, intelligent in practical matters, planning for future

Proverbs 18:15

1. Does the prudent one seek wisdom? ________________

Proverbs 12:16

2. Is a prudent man quick to react to problems?__________

Proverbs 12:23

3. Would "cautious" be a good word to describe a prudent man by? ____

Proverbs 12:23

4. Does a prudent man brag of what he knows?

____

Proverbs 12:23

5. Is it prudent or wise to try to show or tell others how much knowledge we have? ____________________

Proverbs 12:16 & 23

6. Name two things a prudent man "conceals". ____

Proverbs 12:23

7. If you have information that you know another needs, such as how to be saved, or why someone is acting wrongly, should you always share it with them? _______

____

Proverbs13:16

8. Does a prudent man know when to speak and when to be silent? ____________________

Proverbs 14:8

9. Is a prudent man careful to consider how he acts andspeaks or does he fool himself into thinking he can live however he wants to? _______________________________

____

Proverbs 14:15

10. Would a prudent man act upon information before checking himself to see if it was true? ______________

Proverbs 14:18

11. What is God's reward for the prudent? _____________
What about the simple? ____________________________

Proverbs 22:3

12. Is a prudent man cautious of evil? _________________
What is his response to it? __________________________

Proverbs 22:3

13. Would a prudent boy be quick to disobey his parents when playing with his friends, if he thought his parents probably wouldn't know? __________________________

Proverbs 22:3

14. Is it true that a prudent man understands that there are consequences to good and evil that we can't explain?

____

An Example of a Prudent Man

(Crafty)

"Oh, good! Look what Grandma sent me for Christmas!" Jason exclaimed. "It's a nature book, Mom. It tells about lots of animals!"

Mom snapped a picture of Jason holding up his new book with a delighted smile on his face.

"You'll have to look through that with Dad after dinner," she said.

So when everyone had eaten all they could, and when the kitchen was cleaned up and Mom was putting the twins Delores and Dana to bed, Jason took the book from the shelf.

"It's really neat, Dad. It's called ***Wonders of Nature***, and every page has photographs on it," he explained. "Here's the first page of pictures."

Squirrels were on that page, and it showed them gathering food for winter. One of them was hiding nuts in his hollow tree home.

"'*Chapter One: Preparing for Winter.* Prudent squirrels prepare for the coming winter,'" Jason read the caption.

After a little while, he saw a picture of ants. Some of them were black and some were red, but they were all carrying crumbs from a bit of cake they'd found on a sidewalk. "'One ant finds something tasty and goes and tells his friends,'" Jason read the caption again. "'Then they all go and carry as much as they can. They save almost all of it for winter.'"

And only a few pages later, it showed muskrats building thicker houses, preparing for a harder winter than usual, and horses growing more hair in the fall.

"Look at all those animals who are getting ready for the cold weather," Dad pointed out. He took his Bible from the lamp table and flipped through it, turning to Proverbs 27. "Verse 12 says, 'A prudent man forseeth evil and hideth himself...'," he said, explaining, "That's what all these animals are doing. People could learn a great deal from animals if only they'd study them for a little while. They could learn from the little creatures how to be prudent in the same way, preparing for future problems and needs."

Jason nodded. "I see," he said. "Now I think I know how to avoid the future problem of making Grandma think that I don't like this book. I'm going to write her a thank-you note right now, before I have a chance to forget!"

Application Questions

1. What might a prudent man do to get his home or car ready for winter?

2. Name two animals that show prudence.

3. What could happen to a boy who was not prudent while riding his bike?

Fun Quiz

	True	False
1. A prudent person is not quick to talk about shameful things.	_______	_______
2. He loves to tell how much he knows.	_______	_______
3. He acts without getting the facts first.	_______	_______
4. He watches where he is going	_______	_______
5. He prepares in advance for future needs.	_______	_______
6. He is often taken by surprise because of carelessness.	_______	_______

The prudent are crowned with knowledge.

Prov. 14:18

Answers to Fun Quiz:

1. True
2. False
3. False
4. True
5. True
6. False

The Wise Man

(Hebrew *chakun* - "skillful")

Proverbs 1:5

1. Is a wise man quick to listen to Godly counsel? _______

2. Does he learn from counsel, or does he go on and do what he wants to do? ______________________________
____

Proverbs 3:7

3. Does a wise man think he is wise?

____

4. What are two characteristics of the wise man found in this verse? a)_________________________________
b)____

Proverbs 3:35

5. What will be the inheritance of the wise person? ______
____
____

6. What, in contrast, is the fool's reward? ______________

____

Proverbs 6:6

7. What animal will help the sluggard to obtain wisdom?

____

____

Proverbs 8:33

8. How does God specifically tell us to handle instruction?

____

____

9. What will be the result in our lives?

____

____

Proverbs 9:8

10. How will a wise man respond if you rebuke him?

____

____

____

11. Should you rebuke a wise man? ________________

12. How will the scorner respond when rebuked?

____

____

Proverbs 9:9

13. What should we do to help a wise man to be wiser?

____

____

14. Is giving instruction to a wise man a wise thing to do?

____

Proverbs 10:1

15. How does a wise man's father feel?

____

16. How does the mother of a fool feel? ______________

____

Proverbs 10:8

17. Is a wise son or daughter quick or slow to obey their parent's instructions? ____________________________

Proverbs 11:29

18. Is the wise man going to end up as a leader or a servant? ______________________________

19. Who shall be servant to the wise man? ____________

____

Proverbs 11:30

20. What is one characteristic of the wise man, as told in this verse?

____

21. What is another characteristic of the wise person in this verse? ______________________________

Proverbs 12:18

22. What do the words of the wise bring?

____

Proverbs 13:1

23. What do we know about a wise son from this verse?

____

____

Proverbs 13:14

24. When the wise man obeys the rules set for him, what does he escape?

____

Proverbs 13:20

25. What kind of friends should we choose if we wish to be wise?

____

26. What will happen to the companion of fools?

____

____

Proverbs 14:3

27. Does the wise man have a big problem with pride?

____

Proverbs 14:16

28. Who does the wise man fear? ____________________

20. What does this keep him from? ___________________

30. What are two characteristics of the fool, in contrast?

____

____

Proverbs 14:24

31. What is the crown of the wise?

____

Proverbs 15:2

32. What about their words makes it easy to distinguish between a wise man and a fool?

____

____

Proverbs 15:7

33. Does the wise man keep his wisdom bottled up inside himself or does he share it with others? ____________________

____

Proverbs 15:12

34. Will the scorner go to the wise man to learn from him?

____

Proverbs 15:20

35. How does a foolish man feel about his mother? ______

____

36. What does the wise man bring about in the life of his father? ____________________________________

Proverbs 15:31

37. What is the characteristic of the wise person found in this verse? __________________________________

Proverbs 16:14

38. How does a wise man handle the wrath of a king? ____

____

Proverbs 16:21

39. What is another name for the wise in heart? _________

____

40. How can we say things in such a way as to help others listen to us? ________________________________

____

Proverbs 16:23

41. What do we know about the heart, mouth and lips of the wise person?

____

____

Proverbs 17:28

42. Does a wise man want to talk all the time? __________

____

43. Are there times when we should be quiet? __________

Proverbs 18:15

44. What does the wise man seek? ______________________

____

45. Do you think the wise boy or girl uses caution in what they let themselves listen to? ______________________

Proverbs 19:20

46. What does God tell us we should do, so that we will be wise when we are older? ______________________

____

47. What, according to this verse, characterizes a person as being unwise? ______________________

____

Proverbs 20:26

48. What does a wise ruler do to the wicked men under him?______________________

Proverbs 21:11

49. What response does the wise person have when instructed? ______________________

50. What causes the simple fool to be made wise? _______

____

____

Proverbs 21:20

51. What has a wise man learned to do with his money or resources? ____________________________________

Proverbs 21:22

52. How does a wise man approach those mighty in the world's eyes? ___________________________________
Or one stupid in wrong philosophies? ________________

____

Proverbs 22:17

53. What instruction does God give us in His Word concerning the words of the wise? ____________________

____

____

54. What causes a father's heart to rejoice?

____

____

Proverbs 23:19

55. How can a son or daughter help to guide their heart in the way it should go? ______________________________

____

Proverbs 23:24

56. What fruit of the spirit does a wise son bring to his mother and father? (See Galatians 5:22 & 23 if you need to, for the Fruit of the Spirit.) ___________________________

____

Proverbs 24:5

57. How does God describe the wise man in this verse? ___

____

____

____

Proverbs 24:23

58. Would a wise man, if he were a judge, be more likely to decide in the favor of a rich and popular man over a poor man? ____

____

Proverbs 25:12

59. Is an obedient boy or girl glad for a wise reproof?

____

Proverbs 26:5

60. How should we answer a foolish man? ____________

____

61. If we don't answer him wisely, how will he respond?

____

____

Proverbs 27:11

62. What can a son or daughter do to help his/her dad have the authority to answer his enemies, or those who reproach him? ______________________________________

____

Proverbs 28:7

63. What is a characteristic of a wise son in this verse?

____

____

64. What happens to the father of a person who keeps company with riotous people?

____

____

Proverbs 11:11

65. What do scornful men bring about in a city?

____

66. In contrast, what does Scripture tell us about the wise man?

____

____

Proverbs 29:9

67. What happens if a wise man contends with a foolish man?

____

____

Proverbs 29:11

68. Does a wise man quickly say everything he is thinking?

____

Proverbs 30:24-28

69. What 4 little things upon the earth are exceedingly wise?

____

____

____

70. Why are each of the four wise, according to Scripture?

____

____

____

____

An Example of a Wise Man

"Hey, Dad?"

"Mm-hmm?"

"I'm working on a science poster for school. I've got a question."

"What's that, James?" Mr. Gibson put down his newspaper.

"Well, first of all, the project is about matter and motion. How would you explain what the cell is?"

"It's a structural unit of living matter; all living things are composed of cells. The cell is the functional unit of living matter. The smallest part of a living thing which can be considered to be alive is the cell. All cells come from pre-existing cells; living things don't come from nonliving things, you know."

James whistled. "Whew! How did you learn so much about science, Dad?"

Mr. Gibson laughed. "My friends started doing a lot of stuff that I didn't like when I was a little older than you are, James, and I didn't want to get involved. My friend Mr. Peakon was an old retired neighbor of ours, and he did a lot of fun things with me. He took me fishing every other Saturday, took me to museums and amusement parks, and things like that. We talked for hours and hours at a time about things, especially science. We did lots of experiments and read lots of books in the summer about science. That's how I learned so much, and I learned just about all of the science stuff in the summer. Meanwhile, my friends were in a really rough group and wasted all their time getting in trouble. As Mr. Peakon used to say, when he'd see all my friends getting in trouble, 'Lie down with the dogs and you get up with fleas,' and then he'd quote Proverbs 13:20, which says, 'He that walketh with wise men shall be wise, but the companion of fools shall suffer harm.' And one night, those foolish boys I was acquainted with did suffer harm. They did something they shouldn't have—I forget what it was—and all of them had to spend the night in jail. In the morning, their parents had to pay a big fine because their sons didn't have enough money to. They had to work for weeks to pay their parents back."

James whistled again. "Wow! I'll bet you were glad you hadn't been with the gang when that happened."

"I sure was," his dad answered. "I was really glad Mr. Peakon took time to teach me all that, and to take my mind off those other boys who were doing stuff that shouldn't be done. Walk with wise men and you'll grow wise, too."

Application Questions

1. Why do you think some people don't want to ask advice from a wise man?

2. Why do you think the Bible says it is better to have wisdom than to be rich?

3. What are some ways by which you can learn more wisdom?

Fun Quiz

If a sentence is true about a wise man, put an **X** under **"TRUE."** If it isn't, put an **X** under **"FALSE."**

	True	False
1. He listens to learn.	_______	_______
2. A sluggard can learn wisdom from an ant.	_______	_______
3. He will get angry if you try to rebuke him.	_______	_______
4. Fools will become his servants.	_______	_______
5. He speaks harshly.	_______	_______
6. Wisdom doesn't just "rub off" from wise people	_______	_______
7. A wise man is rich	_______	_______
8. Scorners need wisdom and so seek out wise people	_______	_______
9. You have to learn wisdom by experience. You can't learn it from others.	_______	_______

Answers to Fun Quiz

1. True
2. True
3. False
4. True
5. False
6. False
7. True
8. False
9. False

A wise son makes a glad father.

Prov. 15:20

LIAR/FAITHFUL WITNESS

Proverbs 17:4

1. What does a liar like to listen to? ____________________

____

2. Who likes to listen to false or lying lips?

____

Proverbs 19:22

3. Does scripture say it would be better to be poor or to be a liar?

____

4. Therefore, should you ever lie to gain money? _________

5. Instead, what should we desire to be toward others?

____

Proverbs 30:6

6. Why should we guard against ever adding to God's Word?

____

____

(*Another name for a liar, in Proverbs, is a ***false witness***.*)

Proverbs 6:19

7. A false witness, as this verse tells us, speaks __________ ____.

Proverbs 6:16-19

8. In these verses, list the seven things God hates.

a. ____
b. ____
c. ____
d. ____
e. ____
f. ____
g. ____

9. How many of these things involve lying? _________ ____

Proverbs 12:17

10. In this verse, we are told that a liar or false witness speaks with ____________________________________.

Proverbs 14:5

11. What is the difference between a faithful witness and a false witness? ________________________________

____

Proverbs 14:25

12. We are told that the deceitful witness speaks lies. What does a truthful witness do? ________________________

____

____

Proverbs 19:5

13. What will happen to the false witness? ____________

____

____

Proverbs 19:28

14. How does the ungodly witness respond to judgment?

____

____

Proverbs 21:28

15. What else will happen to the false witness? __________

____

____

Proverbs 24:28

16. What does this verse warn us never to do? ___________

____

____

Proverbs 25:18

17. How does God describe one who lies about his neighbor?

a. ____

b. ____

c. ____

18. What do all three of these fools have in common?

____

____

Another word for a liar is ***deceitful witness****. Deceit, according to the dictionary definition, means the act of deceiving, or perversion of the truth for the purpose of misleading; fraud; cheating.*

Proverbs 12:5

19. What kind of counsel would a wicked person give us?

____

____

20. What are the thoughts of the righteous like, in contrast?

____

____

____

Proverbs 12:20

21. What does a person with deceit in his heart think about?

____

____

Proverbs 14:8

22. The prudent wants to understand his way. What are we told about the liar in this verse?

a. ______________________________________

____

b. ______________________________________

____

c. ______________________________________

Proverbs 26:26

23. The liar's deceit is covering up his _______________.

24. What is another thing we are told will happen to the liar?

____

____

Proverbs 20:17

25. Does a liar enjoy lying at first? ___________________

26. How does it affect him afterwards?

____

____

Proverbs 23:3

27. What are we told is deceitful meat? What should we avoid?

____

____

Proverbs 11:18

28. What kind of person works deceitful works?

____

Proverbs 27:6

29. We are told to beware of compliments from an enemy. Why? ________________________________

____

Proverbs 31:30

30. What are we told is deceitful in this verse?

____

31. What should a girl or woman make as her goal? _____

____

____

Proverbs 29:12

32. What happens when a ruler listens to lies?

____

____

Proverbs 12:22

33. How does God feel about lying lips? ______________

____

____

Proverbs 26:18, 19

34. What does God compare one to who lies about his neighbor and then says he was only joking?

____

____

____

Proverbs 20:1

35. What substance can influence someone to be deceived?

____

____

36. What does God say about one who allows himself to be influenced by it? ______________________________

____

____

____

Proverbs 13:17

37. What happens to a wicked messenger? ____________

____

____

____

Proverbs 12:20

38. What is in the heart of those who imagine evil? ______

____

39. What is given to those who are counsellors of peace?

____

____

Proverbs 13:17

40. Is it important to send a faithful person to deliver a message for you? ____________________________

41. What does the Bible say a faithful messenger is?

____

____

Proverbs 14:5

42. What won't a faithful witness do?

____

____

____

Proverbs 20:6

43. Is it easy to find a really faithful person?

____

44. Do most people claim to be honest?

____

Proverbs 25:13

45. What does a faithful messenger do for the soul of his masters, or those who send him? ____________________

____

____

Proverbs 11:13

46. What does one with a faithful spirit do when he hears secrets about others? ________________________________

____

Proverbs 28:20

47. How will God reward a faithful man?

____

____

Proverbs 27:5,6

48. Would a true friend lie to his friend to avoid hurting him? ____

____

Proverbs 12:22

49. How does God feel about one who tells the truth? __

____

____

Proverbs 14:25

50. What does a truthful witness accomplish?

____

____

Proverbs 22:21, 22

51. How can we know the truth?

____

____

52. How should we strive to answer people, especially those with authority over us?

____

Proverbs 22:23

52. What are we told to make an effort to buy?

____

Proverbs 20:28

54. What will preserve the king, or anyone, who rules over another?

____

Proverbs 16:6

55. What purges iniquity? ______________________________

56. How does one depart from evil? ____________________

____

Proverbs 14:22

57. What shall be given to them that preserve truth? ______

____

Proverbs 12:19

58. What does God promise for the lip of truth? __________

____

What does He say about the lying tongue? ___________

____

59. Will a boy or girl get away with lying continually?

____

Proverbs 8:7

60. God gave us our mouths. What are we to use them for?

____

____

61. What should we consider an abomination to our lips, as God does also?

____

____

Proverbs 3:3

62. What are we told to bind about our necks? __________

____

____

63. What are we told to write on the table of our hearts?

____

____

64. What does this mean? _________________________

____

65. Do you think God requires us to memorize His Word regarding truthfulness? ___________________________

____

Proverbs 12: 17

66. When we speak truth, what do we show forth?

____

____

67. Does it honor God when we speak the truth? ________

68. Look up John 14:6. What are the 3 names Jesus called himself in this verse?

a. ____________________________

b. ____________________________

c. ____________________________

If Jesus is TRUTH, then we dishonor Him by speaking lies and honor Him by speaking the truth.

An Example of a False Witness

It was a rainy day in 1870. Laura Pinkerton had nothing to do, since her friend Dorothea had canceled the tea party she had been planning on, and Laura was bored.

"Mother, what can I do?" she asked.

Mrs. Pinkerton looked up from her knitting. "Suppose I tell you a story?"

"Hmm... very well, there's nothing better to do."

"This happened when I was a little girl. Do you remember President Lincoln?"

"Of course."

"Well, before he was President, he was a lawyer. One day, a man came to him looking very troubled. 'Mr. Lincoln,' he said, 'a man whom I have never seen before has accused me of committing a crime. I was not in the vicinity he claimed that I was on that night, but I have no actual proof that I wasn't. Can you help me?'

"Abraham Lincoln was honest, you know, so he got exact details from the man and gathered a few books. When the man — for convenience, let's call him Mr. Smith — was taken to court by the other (we'll call him Mr. Wright), Lincoln was ready.

"Mr. Wright stood up to give his account of the story, and the witness said he had seen Mr. Smith do the crime and was certain of his identity, thanks to the bright moonlight. Mr. Lincoln consulted an almanac when the witness was talking, and then showed everyone that there had been no moon on the night of the crime."

"My goodness!" exclaimed Laura. "So they found out that the man was lying?"

"That's right. You know how the Bible says in Proverbs 14:25, 'A true witness delivereth souls, but a false witness speaketh lies'? Here is just one of many examples of that. A faithful witness would have 'delivered' the defendant, while the false witness spoke a lie."

Application Questions

1. What are some ways in which a liar could cause problems for others?

2. Do you think it would be easier for a truthful person or a liar to have friends? Why?

3. How would you feel if you learned that someone had been telling lies about you?

Fun Quiz

	Liar	Faithful Witness
1. He's not careful about what he hears	_______	_______
2. It is better to be poor than to be this man	_______	_______
3. You can become one of these by saying more about something than God does	_______	_______
4. He gets people out of trouble	_______	_______
5. He has no respect for judgment	_______	_______
6. He's like a maul, a sword and a sharp arrow	_______	_______
7. He can keep a secret	_______	_______
8. He says he's "just kidding"	_______	_______
9. He shows forth righteousness	_______	_______
10. He helps purge iniquity	_______	_______

Answers to Fun Quiz:

1. Liar
2. Liar
3. Liar
4. Faithful Witness
5. Liar
6. Liar
7. Faithful Witness
8. Liar
9. Faithful Witness
10. Faithful Witness

A faithful witness will not lie.

Prov. 14:5

Also by the Boyers:

NEW!!!! Parenting From the Heart
Marilyn, a mother of 14 with over 30 years experience, shares her heart with you in this, her newest release, *Parenting From the Heart.* You can raise godly children! It's a matter of accepting a God-given calling and pursuing it by His principles. It is a heart-to-heart relationship in which children are not just trained but discipled. Some chapter titles:
So Now You're a Mommy!
Gotta Love Those Toddlers!
God Made You Special for a Special Purpose
Building a Heart of Obedience
Saturate Your Home With Scripture
Guard Their Hearts
Turning Problems Into Projects
Standing Alone
Give Them Your Heart
From Sorrow to Joy
What Home Education Did for Our Family
What Are We Working For, Anyway?
From My Heart to Yours
$12.95

The Hands-On Dad
Rick shares seven Biblical functions for the father and shows how they apply in home education. These important and practical insights can set both Mom and Dad free to be the best for their children. **$9.95**

Home Educating With Confidence
Rick and Marilyn Boyer share their experiences to encourage and equip others. You don't have to be a child psychologist or have a fancy degree to raise godly children. **$10.95**

Fun Projects for Hands-On Character Building
The Boyers share their philosophy of spiritual training with scores of practical, effective, and enjoyable projects. **$9.95**

Yes, They're All Ours
The story of the Boyer family – what life is like with 14 children, and why we chose to live this way. Also includes humorous anecdotes. **$9.95**

Homemade with Love
Marilyn Boyer shares her tried and true recipes for feeding 14 children economically and simply. **$9.95**

The Runt
Rick Boyer shares with young readers the fictional adventures of a boy and his uncompromising mongrel pup. With that scrap of a dog, God teaches what it really means to be a winner. **$9.95**

The Socialization Trap
Most home educators reject school for their children partly because of damaging pressures from age-peer social groups. Yet many parents try to replace lost "social contact" by placing their children in age-graded activities that re-create the peer pressure all over again. This book tells why you don't need to! This is the answer you need to the question, "What about socialization?" **$8.95**

<u>Bible Curriculum</u>
Character Qualities Flashcards
Cards feature a question and picture to color on the front, and a verse on the back. For example: "Why should we choose godly friends?" Answer: "He who walks with wise men shall be wise, but the companion of fools will be destroyed." Proverbs 13:20 **$5.00**

If/When Flashcards
Teach your children what to do in certain situations. For example: "When tempted to hate correction (Prov. 12:1)?" Answer: "Whoever loves discipline loves knowledge, but he who hates reproof is stupid." **$5.00**

Proverbs Flashcards
Teach your children Bible verses from the Book of Wisdom. Each card features a picture for your child to color. **$5.00**

Proverbs for Preschoolers
Children learn the principles in Proverbs while practicing stylus skills, memorizing the alphabet, and coloring. **$12.95**

Proverbs People I & II
Workbooks that use short-answer questions, stories, quizzes, and coloring pages to teach character qualities to children 8 to 12. **$15.00 ea.**

Living the Fruitful Life
A Bible study course on how to apply the fruit of the Spirit to our lives. For middle-school students. **$15.00**

Power in Proverbs
A self-led concordance study guide for teenagers. **$10.95**

Cassette Presentations:
Uncle Rick Reads the Proverbs
Rick Boyer reads the book of Proverbs to kids. (Recommended for children ages 3-12) 5 Hours **Cass. $19.95 CD $24.95**

Uncle Rick Reads the Gospel of Matthew
Cass. $15.00 CD $19.95

Uncle Rick Reads His Favorite Psalms
Cass. $15.00 CD $19.95Proverbs

Uncle Rick Tells Bible Stories Vol. 1
Cass. $10.00 CD $12.00

Uncle Rick Tells Bible Stories Vol. 2
Cass. $10.00 CD $12.00

Memory Tapes
The entire book of Proverbs on two sixty-minute cassettes. **Cass. $10.00 CD $12.00**

Single Tapes:
By Rick Boyer
Dad – Leader in the Home
The Father's role in home education

What About Socialization?

Raising Cain Without Killing Abel
(Sibling Rivalry)

Proverbs: God's Character Curriculum

Child Discipline

Home Educating With Confidence

Careers Without College

Making Learning Fun

Home Educating With Confidence

Some Things We've Learned Over 22 Years of Homeschooling

Reclaiming the American Vision

Beyond the Textbooks

Heroes – Standing on the Shoulders of Giants

The Homeschooling Family and the Church

What Is Education?

Cass. $5.00 ea.
CD $6.00 ea.

By Marilyn Boyer:
Hands-On Character Building

Parenting From the Heart

Home Educating With Babies and Toddlers and Loving It

Home Education – What It's Done for Our Family

Getting It All Done

Cass. $5.00 ea.
CD $6.00 ea.

To request a free catalog of the previous books as well as a whole range of Christian home school materials, please contact the Learning Parent at:

(434) 845-8345
2430 Sunnymeade Road
Rustburg, VA 24588
www.thelearningparent.com